I Never Promised You a Rose Garden

MANNIE MURPHY

FANTAGRAPHICS BOOKS   SEATTLE, WASHINGTON

FANTAGRAPHICS BOOKS INC.
7563 Lake City Way NE
Seattle, Washington, 98115
www.fantagraphics.com

Editor and Associate Publisher: Eric Reynolds
Book Design: Justin Allan-Spencer
Production: Paul Baresh & Christina Hwang
Publisher: Gary Groth

ISBN 978-1-68396-410-0
Library of Congress Control Number 2020942306

First printing: March 2021
Printed in China

I Never Promised You a Rose Garden

MANNIE MURPHY

MANNIE MURPHY

CHAPTER 1

My Own
Private Portland

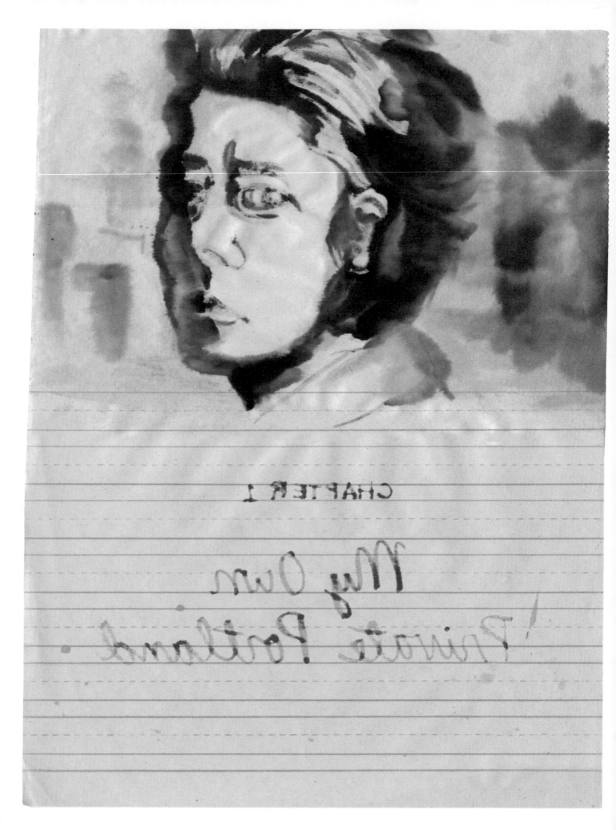

CHAPTER 1

*My Own
Private Portland.*

It was 21 years ago
this Halloween
that we learned the
terrible news.

Alder's mom yelled to **us**
from the top of the stairs.
Calling, repeating, calling,
repeating: River Phoenix
was dead of a heroin overdose.

On the Sunset Strip,
River lay dying in front
of **his** brother, sister,
girlfriend, **and** countless
costumed revelers.

River had caught the world's attention only a few years prior with his portrayal of the troubled Chris Chambers in the film adaptation of Stephen King's "The Body".

Several short, fiery years later and he was gone like a comet, lying on the ground outside of Johnny Depp's **Viper Room**.

River was stunning.
One part James Dean,
   two parts Sal Mineo,
there was something in his
hard stare that said fear,
bravery, and life-lust.

His vibrance radiated out from the screen.

When I first saw Chris Chambers' tearful campfire confession, I was done for.

As River grew, so did
his infamy.
Sultry, brooding, sensitive
and passionate,
his eyes were like magnets.

"Explorers"..."Stand By Me"...
"Mosquito Coast"..."Young
Indiana Jones"... All these
would pale in comparison to his
portrayal of queer narcoleptic street
hustler Mike in "My Own Private Idaho."

River teamed up with buddy Keanu for the lead, **walking** on air to be working with his idol Gus Van Sant in this street epic loosely based on Shakespeare's "Henry V."

Gus fancied troubled boys.
The ones with the eyes older
than their faces.
        The ones with stories
to tell. Secrets.

River surely had stories but he wasn't one to keep them secret. **Born in Oregon**, raised in a cult, River emigrated to Costa Rica where he and his brothers and **sisters** were left to fend for themselves.

River, Rain, and Joaquin grew up on the streets and supported their family busking. He had a total **lack** of pop culture influencing his youth, but there was drugs and sex— both **of** which came too early.

River's combination of hard-
scrabble survival, emotional
intelligence, and good looks
made him irresistable to
other boys and men.

One of these man-crushes
was Keanu. Gus must have
recognized their chemistry immediately.
He set to work on a collaborative
script inspired and **deeply influenced**
by River and his tumultuous life.

Keanu was from the hill, and
River was from the streets—that's
how Gus put it. They were an
"odd couple," and as screen stars
they competed for attention with a
third star of the film: the city of Portland.

THE COMING OF
THE WHITE MAN

Gus has a weakness for obsessive, unrequited love stories, and as a Portland boy, his racial sensitivity is sorely lacking (see: "Mala Noche"). The above statement (dressing an actor as an 'Indian' atop the elk statue, with a plaque reading "the coming of the white man") is about as close as he gets

River and Keanu sank into a
Portland out of time — relatively un-
changed for a century.

    The rainy gritty grey city
attracted street kids from all over
the N.W.

    The winters are relatively mild;
    there was a sex shop on nearly
every block, and johns a-plenty.

Gus was friendly with many of these young men.

Their lives, interpersonal dramas, and tribulations were the stuff of dreams for this rich kid from the Portland Hills.

He interviewed these slick wordsmiths and put them in his movies.

I always cringe
during this scene in "Idaho."
Gus presses his leading
lads for information about
their first and worst dates.

Theirs is a subculture
unmentioned in Portland (polite)
company. The 'vice districts' and
underground economies are rooted in
the fertile soil. Portland became
known for its sex industry as a place
where boys could trade their bodies to men
for $$$

LOVE
USCLE

STUP

LACK
BELT

TORSO
KING
LEER

H

Many of the young men earning their living this way are 'straight-looking and acting'. They consider themselves straight.

This is exactly how Gus likes them.

River was a different story. His characteristic naiveté **allowed** him to overlook certain social mores, and he saw nothing threatening in identifying openly as bisexual.

Keanu, homo not-so-much.
Though he and River had an
undeniable connection. When asked
by "Interview" if he'd do more Shakespeare,
Keanu answers, "maybe 'A Midsummer
Night's Dream' or 'Romeo and Juliet.'"
River interjects, "I'll be Juliet."

But thankfully Gus was able to work in plenty of bro-on-bro action all the same.

One scene that caused much
tension both behind and in
front of the camera was **the** campfire scene. Nobody really knew what
River was going **to do** — **not Gus,**
not Keanu.

River always looks so damn good
by firelight. He confesses his love for
Keanu. "I really wanna kiss you man,"
he says.

At this, Keanu "no homo" Reeves
pulls drunk River into an
embrace.
　　Did River go in for a kiss
only to have Keanu turn from him
in the last seconds of the take?
　　It's hard to tell.
Gus must have been head over
　　heels in love.

The most compelling evidence to support this theory is the book "Pink," by Van Sant. The main character (who closely resembles Gus) attempts to cope with the death of Felix (closely resembling River) by hooking up with a guy who reminds him of River— I mean, Felix.

I think Gus fancied himself a modern version of his boy-loving, woman-hating, smack-shooting idol, William S. Burroughs.

Gus situated himself as the
head, or leader, of his street family
of hunky boys. River, Keanu, and
the others moved into Gus' Goose
Hollow home. There were late nights
there, and liberal heroin use.
    River's first time shooting
up was during this stay in Portland.

The boys absolutely adored Gus, with his money and his camera. He earned their loyalty. It was a mutually beneficial situation.

Heroin was a big part of Portland street life. Not so much now since the meth seeped in and took over.

But heroin is still cheaper and easier to get here than weed. Gus made heroin a significant player in his film "Drugstore Cowboy."

Gus had a favorite hunting ground for finding boys and girls (mostly boys) for his films in the '80s, and that was my school; M.L.C.*

A K-12 school for misfits and dropouts. Street wise tough kids waiting for Gus to make them a star.

* Metropolitan Learning Center

MLC was connected by a giant city block to Couch Park (pronounced: "cootch").

Couch Park was a well-known cruising ground, complete with public bathrooms, bushes, and a rad play structure that provided private nooks and **crannies** for shooting up, *or fucking*.

A lot of street kids hung out at M.L.C. It was a lax, loose, minimally supervised environment modeled after the book "Summerhill." "It was a den of sin, or a sanctuary depending on how you looked at it. The place attracted punks and queers, who **naturally** attracted Gus.

Many never made it out of Portland. They wound up in the Willamette River, or under the suicide Bridge,

on a gurney with a swollen arm,
in front of a speeding train.

The pharmacy across the
street from M.L.C. was the setting
for the opening scene in
"Drugstore Cowboy";
    the one where Heather
Graham fakes a seizure
while Matt Dillon ransacks
the pharmaceuticals.

Matt Dillon's character Bob closely resembled real-life street kid, infamous neo nazi, and Gus' pal Ken Death. Unbeknownst to us, Bob seemed the epitome of cool.

My buddies and I would fight
over the privilege to sip from the
exact fountain Matt Dillon
drinks from just before
the heist, located between our
school and our lunchspot,
The Thriftee Deli.

We plastered our faces
to the school windows as we
watched Matt Dillon repeatedly
peel out of our parking lot
    the wrong way, down a one-way
street in the getaway car.

Unlike fictitious Bob, reality
never set in for River.
Instead of blissful sleep, it
was violent seizures and heartbreak.

It was Joaquin's desperate
pleas shattering the nightly news-
cast, we heard him for the first time
saying, "It's my brother. Please come.
He's dying. Please."

And while Gus painted
this strange picture of heroin
as a blissful, sub-urban dream,
We all knew
it could not
end well.

Gus, you know,
has a penchant
for the tragic.
His trio "Elephant," "Last Days,"
and "Gerry" were dubbed
the "Death" series.

"Last Days" of course
memorializes the imagined last
days of a rock star whose early
demise 6 months later virtually
swept River's death under
the rug.
        River was my Kurt.
        Not that it's a contest.

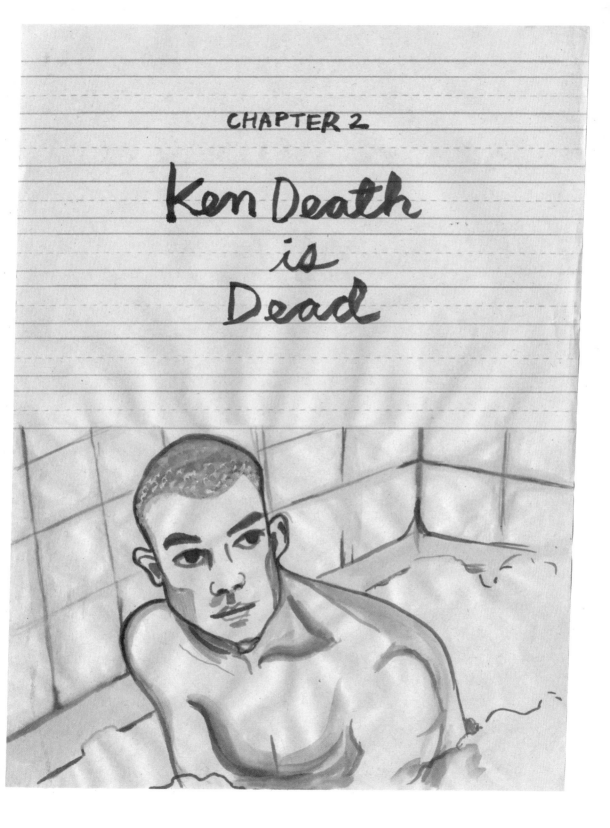

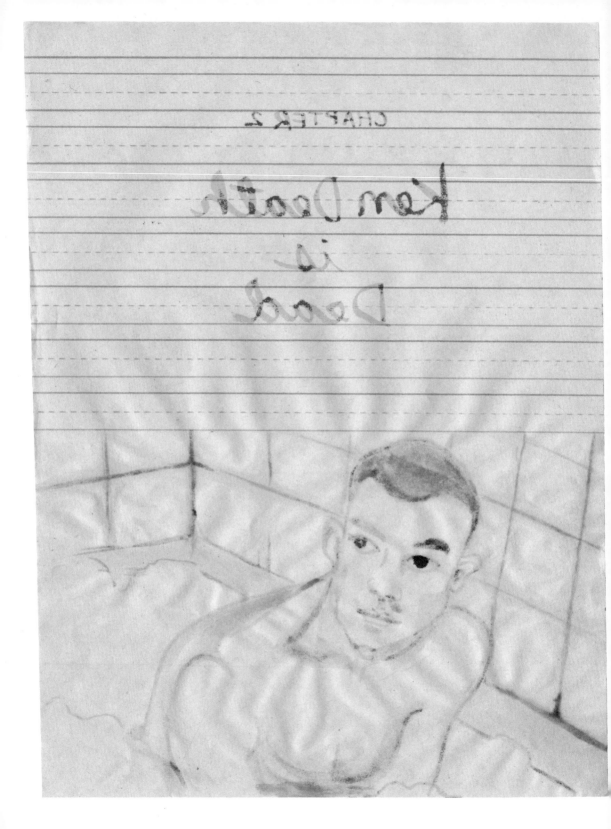

River Phoenix was three years
Kurt's junior. Besides a closeness
in age, the two had other things
in common:
     First, their untimely
deaths were only four months
apart.

Second, they each picked up a guitar at an early age and never put it down.

River toured with his band, Aleka's Attic. He was planning to hop onstage and jam with friends at the Viper Room the night he died.

Third, they were both born in dreary, desolate, Pacific North-western towns. Kurt Cobain in the misty gloom of Aberdeen, WA on the Olympic Peninsula. River, under the big sky, amongst the sagebrush in Madras, Oregon.

He would return to Madras later to film the opening sequences in "My Own Private Idaho." But there was never anywhere River truly considered "home".

The Phoenix brood was bred
in the shadow of a cult
called "Children of God." The
parents moved their growing
family out of the country in
1975 to continue their goal
of winning converts over
to the sect of their charis-
matic leader, David Brandt Berg,
or, "Moses."

River and his guitar and
his sister Rain brought
home the bacon ~ though
not literally. The two became
known locally as "Los Minos
Rubios Que Cantan", or "The
Blonde Children Who Sing".

River's life wasn't a bed of roses. He saw reality in a brutal, illuminating light. This awareness inclined young River towards animal rights. His family went vegan to support River's efforts; they considered him their own personal prophet.

People For The Ethical Treatment Of Animals

But too fast is too fast, even for a prophet. The Children of God encouraged their young to experiment sexually with adults and other children. Later in an interview, River would profess that he "lost his virginity" at age four.

But he had a keen sense of
self~awareness. He knew his
early experiences had taken
their toll. Later he would
confess to losing his "true
virginity" while on location
for the filming of the 1980s
coming~of~age classic, "Stand
By Me."

Encouraged to become fast friends
for the movie, River and his three
co-stars threw themselves into the task,
exploring the back roads and dive
bars of rural Oregon. There they met
some local teenagers who were impressed—
but not so impressed as to keep them
from inviting the stars to party. River
would get stoned, drunk, & laid~ all for
the first time in rural Oregon.

Director Rob Reiner prepped River for his big scene by the campfire: "Is there a moment in your life," he asked River, "when you can recall an adult betraying you in some way? You don't have to tell me who it is. I just want you to think about it." And the result is one of the most raw, moving performances I had ever seen.

River's friends knew he was different. They knew his life had been hard. They never really knew what was going on in his brain or what was going to come out of his mouth at any given moment. But River was loveable. And oh! How they loved him.

The summer months with the "Stand By Me" boys was the first time he'd really make friends outside his family. The next time he would achieve this level of intimacy would again be in Oregon ~ years later in Gus's house on the hill.

River, Keanu, Flea, and all the rent boys and hustlers who became mentors for their roles in "My Own Private Idaho," all began living ~ and partying~ in Van Sant's home. River was a devotee of method acting, often very nearly becoming the characters he was giving life to. River sank into his role as the narcoleptic street hustler, "Mike". They visited Vaseline Alley and the Fruit Loop, showed him how to catch Johns.

This new world of wealthy johns, homeless rockers, drug permissiveness, arthouse flicks, radical politics, and very few chicks seemed enticingly familiar yet was still far removed from his past. Ah, Portland. That liberal bastion of beauty and tolerance... a tolerance we would all soon learn was not always a sign of a healthy community.

1988 was the year Gus met and began living with street kid and hustler Michael Parker—the inspiration for River's Mike Waters. In '88, the heart of Portland was cracked open to reveal a facade, shattered by the sound of splintering bone. Mulugeta Seraw had been murdered and the world permanently altered. The denizens of Doomtown went into a state of shock. Or denial. It can be hard to tell the difference.

Seraw, a 27-year-old father and active member of Portland's Ethiopian Immigrant community, was the victim of a hate crime, murdered by a stranger everybody knew. The scene of the crime was a sleepy, close-in neighborhood in the S.E. The killers: 3 skinhead punks from the notorious street gang, East Side White Pride.

The impact of the murder weapon, a baseball bat weilded by the most ruthless of the three ~ Ken "Death" Mieske ~ rang out accross the country. An attempt would be made to affix the blame for this evil deed to the outspoken champion of evil: Tom Metzger. An example would be made. And while this feat would be ultimately successful, there would be a swift and dangerous kickback.

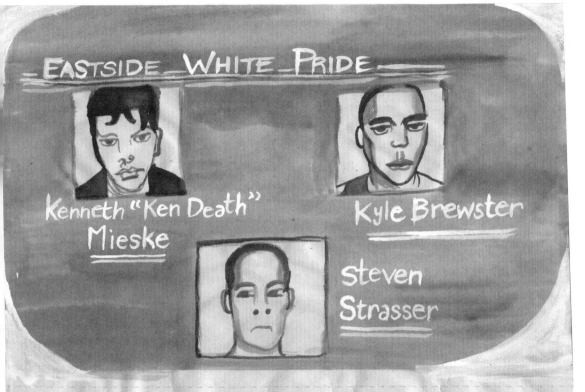

EASTSIDE WHITE PRIDE

Kenneth "Ken Death" Mieske

Kyle Brewster

Steven Strasser

"Ken Death is dead" my roommate called from upstairs. July 2001, she's reading Indymedia. "Good riddance", she says and my muscles tense as I worry that they'll make him a martyr. In 1988 the news spread like a sick~ ness and the naming of the suspects really brought it home: Grant High homecoming King Kyle Brewster; MLC stu~ dent Steve Strasser; and of course, Ken Death.

Ken was already notorious. He was well-
known in Portland's burgeoning underground
punk and deathrock scenes. He was hot-
headed, quick-tempered, and sarcastic.
Not just another nihilistic white boy, this
one was dangerous. And cool, Lord help us.

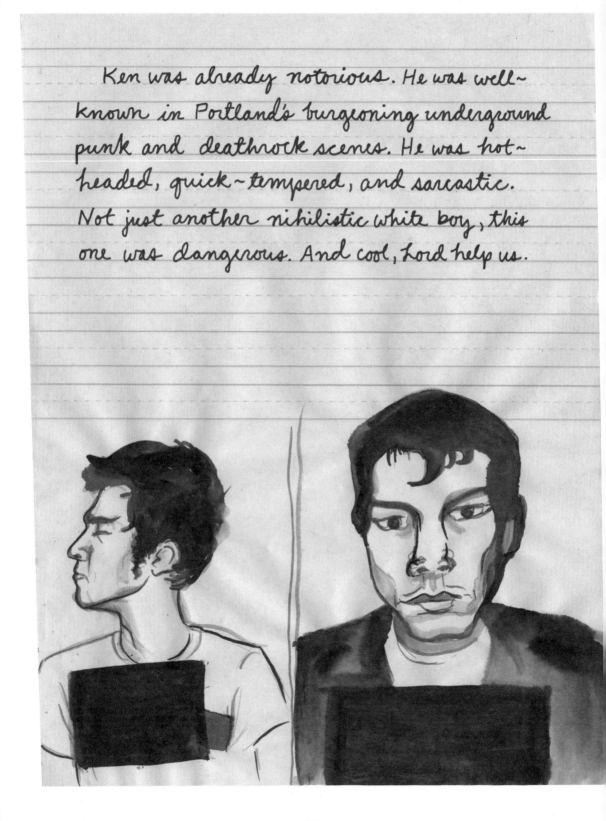

He was just a kid but he com~
manded the respect and attention
of his peers and adults alike. Many
folks, once you get them started,
have Ken Death stories. He didn't
exactly go to my school but he hung
out there a lot.

Gus did finally capture Ken Death on film, a short called, "Ken Death Gets Out of Jail". Ken rambles on in the dark by the side of the highway about how bad he is at fucking. It feels very adlibbed but Gus definitely wrote the script. A few months later, on a night a lot like this one, Ken would commit a heinous murder. He wears his nazi pins in the film, currently locked away in Gus's hidden vault.

Having nothing but the most idyllic childhood himself, Gus was fascinated by these boys and their sordid life stories. He wanted them to be in his movies. He hoped Ken would come to the auditions for "Drugstore Cowboy" but Ken never showed.

Ken was attracted to the skin—head movement, and he fit right in. Skins could be a real pain in the ass ~ especially when they were drunk. But Lord were they sexy! They adopted nazi—esque atten~ tion to fashion. Their aesthetic served both to impress outsiders as well as inspire fear. They were viscerally homoerotic.

The skinhead movement may have ori~ ginated in mixed~race working class/ immigrant communities. People feel all kinds of ways about them. But let's be clear: In the PNW, the skins were the poster boys of the Northwest Territorial Imperative ~ the blossoming conviction that the PNW was an aryan oasis that held the promise of a white homeland like a carrot in front of white nationalists.

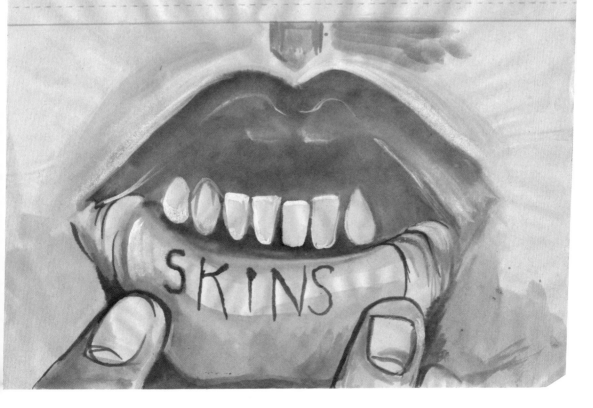

In 1988, the number of militant whites in the Pacific Northwest was ballooning as "nice" white people looked in the other direction. Which didn't change the fact that Oregon was considered to be the most racist state north of the Mason-Dixon line.

I don't know what led fifteen-year-old Kenneth Mieske to get on a train in Seattle bound for Portland. Or how he wound up living in the luxurious West Hills home of gay, ex-cop, entrepreneur Mr. X.

Perhaps it was the need for money
and a roof over his head during the
approaching winter. Maybe it was
Ken's desire for love and attention,
a substitute for a family he'd never
had. Whatever the reason, Mr. X
picked him up outside Portland's Union
Station and moved him into that
house in the hills.

Portland's history of questionably eth- ical man/boy re- lations goes back to its early days as a port town. Sailors down on their luck might get pimped, or crimped and sold out to sea. Some were set up in one of the many riverside boarding houses, accru- ing vast debt, eventually owing their lives to their landlords.

Underground economies sprang up where-
ever it rained and thrived well under the
radar of respectable Portland society. Migrant
workers, homeless homos, street youth, and other
occupants of Doomtown's transient communities
jostle and hustle, at constant risk of exploitation
by more privileged men cruising for their
next mark.

Mr. X owned some of the best punk
clubs in Portland. He set his boy Ken up
with a job on the stage crew at Pine Street
Theater. Pine Street had some good shows.
But heshers, queers, and people of color
had to watch their backs for the nazi
skins who inevitably showed up to
ruin the party, and worse. Much,
much worse.

Mr. X and Gus were tight bros from way back. Mr. X helped to produce Gus's first picture, "Mala Noché" ~ a queer, artsy, racist take on the lives of two seasonal res~ idents of Portland and Mexico, from the perspective of the narcissistic, white, convenience store clerk obsessed with them. Based on Walt Curtis's book by the same name.

Mr. X and Gus knew Ken was special. They found his mix of mannish and boyishness undeniably attractive. Ken Death was becoming kind of an anti-sweetheart in the underground arts and music scene. He didn't give a FUCK and the artists surrounding him were amused and impressed. I have often wondered: where were they when?

The PNW is a place where youth
fall through the cracks and into
the jaws of adults who often know just
where~ and how~ to catch them. The high
numbers of desperate youth combine
with the libertarian ethics of the 'Wild'
West to make the Northwest a goldmine
for white supremacist recruitment.

Neo-nazi recruiters use many of the same tactics to groom their victims as abusers do. They know a mark when they see one.

"Mala Noché" is hailed as a gay cinematic masterpiece... and while it has its moments of beauty, it is also an unfortunate prototype for a specific, Portland breed of hipster racism.

I'm not saying Mr. X and Gus were perpetrating abuse, necessarily. River was a grown-up, he made his own decisions. He and his friends had as much power in this dynamic (owing to what Gus calls the "privilege of youth") as the older men did... right?

The nature of Ken Death's relationship with Mr. X... or River's relationship with Gus... or whether any of these young men were truly masters of their own fate rather than hurtling headlong into the abyss will remain a mystery to me.

HAGGERTY

The murder trial put Portland in the national spotlight for the first time since the Blazers won the championship in '77. Judge Haggerty presided over the courtroom drama ~ and tension so thick you could cut it with a knife ~ as Portland began to get hot under its collective collar.

In a bizarre plot twist, the prose-
cution secured plea deals with the
skinheads by offering a shorter sen-
tence—and in some cases no sentences
at all—in exchange for testimony tying
nationally known white supremacist
Tom Metzger and his son John to the
murder.

Tom Metzger represented himself
in court. In a bold display of white
privilege and arrogance he would spout
his racist ideology throughout the
trial, relying on his right to freedom
of speech to protect him from this leftist plot.

Prosecuting attorney Morris Dees of the Southern Poverty Law Center wanted to bag this big fish. He danced a dangerous dance with the skinheads, making sure to portray them as alternately culpable and incapable; they were Lost Boys taken under the wing of Captain Hook. San Diego resident and radio talk-show host Tom Metzger was the prize, and Dees readied the trap to snare him in.

Some chilling testimony came while Dees was interviewing Ken Death as a hostile witness: Mieske decribes in painfully glib detail how he brought his bat against Seraw's temple, using his mic to demonstrate. Years later his pals still referred to him as Batman.

A terrifying thought was dawning on some of our minds: what if this ~ the media attention, the expression of their ideals under the duress of liberal forces ~ was exactly what they wanted? What if that was the point? Would they be mar~ tyred? Because they were starting to look like celebrities.

Morris Dees's prize player in the takedown of Metzger was Ken Death ~ who played the role of the hateful psychopath flawlessly because he wasn't acting. But Dees's secret weapon, the final nail in the Metzger's coffin, was Metzger's very own protegé, Dave Mazella.

Dave Mazella was the leader of a ragtag gang, the Southern Oregon skins. After a phase of violence and mayhem, it is likely that Mazella got busted and turned rat. As vice president of the Aryan Youth Movement, he had regular dealings with the Metzgers. At Dees's prompting, Mazella turned triple-agent, Keeping Dees in the loop as he brought the Metzgers and the skins of ESWP together.

Mazella was credited as the main person driving the Portland skins to racial violence, but he never did time for any of his many crimes (Mazella, above left).

Largely incoherent and in visible shock from the Mazella reveal, Metzger fumbled through testimony as he cross-examined himself in the third person. But he picked up steam as the 40-hour trial progressed.

Tom's son, John Metzger, was the so-called president of the Aryan Youth Movement. He had fashioned a tidy, professional look for himself, in contrast with the skinheads. He was more articulate and confident than his father. He was more comfortable under the microscope and in front of the camera. This was likely from his previous experiences on "Oprah," "Geraldo," and "Sally."

It was the eighties: the media train was rumbling along and skinheads were HOT. When John Metzger appeared on "Geraldo" a mere ten days before the Seraw murder, he purposefully started an on-air riot which left the host bloodied with a broken nose from a flying chair. This was reality TV in its teen years and like Geraldo said later: it was good television.

Metzger's "Oprah" appearance also became infamous. Oprah was called a racist slur by a knucklehead in the audience. Later she said she regretted ever giving them a national audience for their hateful messages. John Metzger and Dave Mazella were guests onstage, while Tom Metzger hid in the audience.

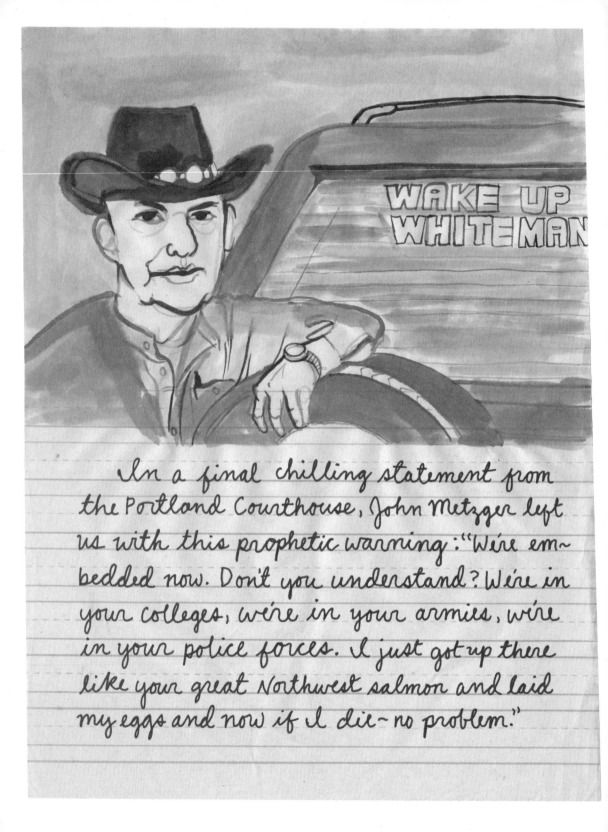

In a final chilling statement from the Portland Courthouse, John Metzger left us with this prophetic warning: "We're embedded now. Don't you understand? We're in your colleges, we're in your armies, we're in your police forces. I just got up there like your great Northwest salmon and laid my eggs and now if I die - no problem."

CHAPTER 3

Flood

Oregon did not start off well. It began in greed and betrayal, blood and hubris. To understand the origins of Oregon, to see how it became the state it is today, we must return to the scene of the Whitman massacre.

On November 29, 1847, in what was
then Oregon, the missionary Marcus
Whitman, his wife Narcissa, and 11 other
settlers were slaughtered by a small
group of Cayuse. 45 women and children
were taken captive and held for ransom.
What had provoked such utter vengeance
from the neighboring Cayuse?

This monument to whiteness was erected near what is now Walla Walla, Washington, in Oregon Territory where the Wailatpu Mission once stood. The Whitmans, along with their friends the Spaldings, left the East for the Oregon frontier to proselytize to the Nez Perce who, word had it, were interested in the white man's Book of Heaven. The Whitmans of Wailatpu were decidedly less well-received by the Cayuse bands on whose lands they'd settled.

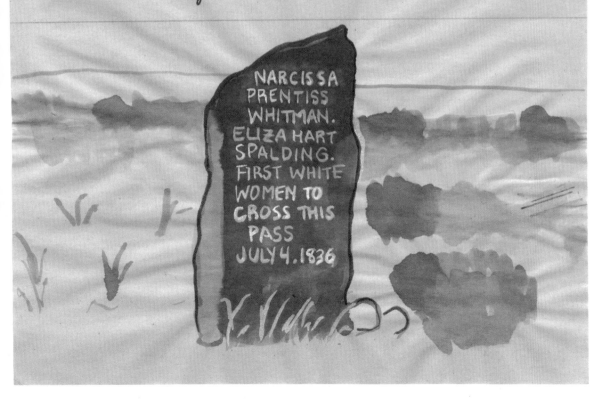

NARCISSA PRENTISS WHITMAN. ELIZA HART SPALDING. FIRST WHITE WOMEN TO CROSS THIS PASS JULY 4. 1836

Marcus Whitman quickly reassessed his priorities. Rather than work administering medical aid and religion to the reluctant Cayuse, he would turn his attentions to ballooning the fledgeling white population in the sparse Oregon Territory. He played travel agent, tour guide, and social worker to waves of immigrants flowing in on the new Oregon Trail. Whitman would ensure those trickling numbers of new Oregonians reached flood proportions.

Whitman reasoned that the Cayuse would not long survive his own people's invasive diseases and land theft and and that the advancement of the white Anglo-Saxon Protestant upon its Native inhabitants was an inevitabity.

Two years after successfully neg-
otiating the release of the Wailatpu
captives, two tribal leaders, Tiloukaikt
and Tomahas, with three more Cayuse
said to be involved in the massacre of
the Whitmans traveled to Oregon City to
speak to their crimes. It is unlikely they
knew they would be tried for murder. Their
lawyer used the defense that it was tribal
law that any doctor practicing bad medicine
be killed. And Marcus Whitman had practiced
bad medicine.

Marcus Whitman and his people gave the Cayuse measles, dyssentery, and other diseases that decimated their population. Dr. Whitman could seemingly cure his own people. Why then not the Cayuse? Whitman and his landmates poisoned meat and melons that the Cayuse had eaten. Whitman spoke openly about the Cayuse's impending demise. He was a bad doctor. The five Cayuse were publicly hanged in Oregon City, just south of Portland.

The Whitman massacre was lev-
eraged against the White House, and
Oregon the state was born. Oregon would
not forget, and anti-Indigenous sen-
timent became embedded into its bylaws
and legislation. This new Oregon would be
made into the white man's utopia Marcus
and Narcissa envisioned. But it wasn't just
the Native inhabitants the new Oregonians
worried about.

White Oregonians worried about losing their white utopia so they tried from the start to keep other groups from settling there. There were laws written into the Oregon constitution specifically forbidding Black people from entering and/or remaining in Oregon. Laws prohibited Chinese and Japanese immigration to Oregon. "Lash" laws terrorized Black people who stayed, threatened with public torture.

Fast forward a few decades to 1915. "Birth of a Nation" is released in movie theaters and Klan fever sweeps the north like a prairie fire. Recruitment was particularly fierce in bastions of whiteness like Oregon. They were embraced as a new modern version of the old Klan: anti~catholic, anti~private schooling, a progressive anglo~Saxon Protestant terrorist organization.

The above photo was taken August 1, 1921.
It shows the Portland police captain and
police chief, the mayor of Portland, a few
district attorneys, a representative of the
Scottish Rite Masons, a King Kleagle, and an
exalted cyclops. This is what city planning
looked like.

Governor Walter Pierce was just one of many Oregon state officials elected by Klan power, having been members themselves. The network of terror was already broad and vast in 1920s Oregon.

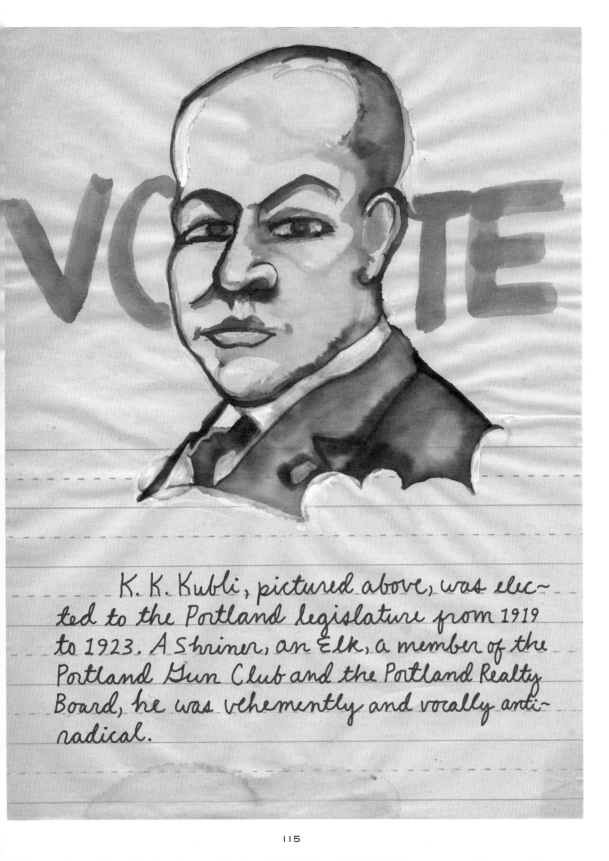

K. K. Kubli, pictured above, was elected to the Portland legislature from 1919 to 1923. A Shriner, an Elk, a member of the Portland Gun Club and the Portland Realty Board, he was vehemently and vocally antiradical.

If you were white in Portland in the 1920s you could do almost whatever you wanted. With a bustling waterfront and law enforcement looking the other way, vice reigned supreme. It must have been an exciting, frightening place.

Bunco Kelly lives on in local memory as a character of the times. He was a crimp, which is like a pimp, only Bunco procured unwitting sailors to ship's captains hungry for unsullied crew members. Young sailors, loggers, hobos, and migrant workers were all fair game to the crimp running out of boarding houses plied to the weary traveler. Men like Bunco are practically hailed as Portland founding fathers.

    In winter 2015~16 the Bundy family and several cohorts decided to occupy federal land in Malheur County, Oregon, to protest the imprisonment of the Hammonds for committing arson on public lands. The armed occupiers vowed that if the Feds were to raid their encampment, it would risk a "conflagration so great, it cannot be stopped, leading to a bloody, brutal civil war."

But what were they doing in Oregon in the first place? Why here? You'll remember Tom Metzger used the metaphor of the salmon returning to spawn to bring home the idea that white supremacy was already embedded in the culture of Portland and the Pacific Northwest. But where did he get this idea?

blue   white   green

He probably got the idea from Richard Butler, Harold Covington, or any other of the white nationalist leaders advocating for a white ethnostate. Covington, the architect of the Northwest Territorial Imperative and the leader of the Northwest Front whose flag is seen above, passed away while I was writing this chapter. Good riddance.

On that flag, "The sky is blue, the earth is green, and white is for the people in between." The flag is eerily similar to the Cascadia flag, seen below. Cascadia is another secession movement claiming the Pacific Northwest bioregion.

blue

white

green

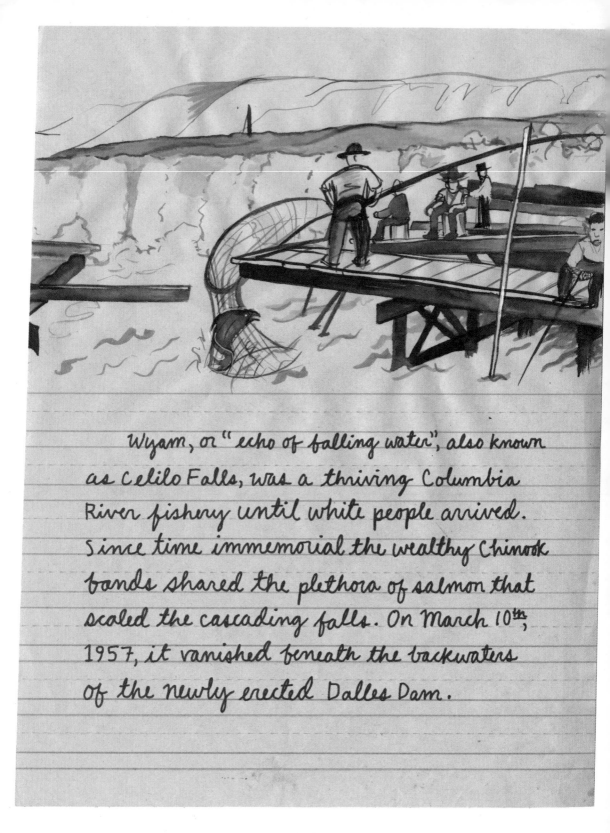

Wyam, or "echo of falling water", also known
as Celilo Falls, was a thriving Columbia
River fishery until white people arrived.
Since time immemorial the wealthy Chinook
bands shared the plethora of salmon that
scaled the cascading falls. On March 10th,
1957, it vanished beneath the backwaters
of the newly erected Dalles Dam.

Archaeologists and private collectors, pros and amateurs alike were allowed to take what they could of the petroglyphs surrounding the sacred site before being subsumed by floodwaters. Precious relics were disseminated into public and private collections. Celilo Village was left destitute. The power from the Dalles Dam made possible the growth of surrounding cities, including Portland.

In 1940s Oregon, a new city was being built to accommodate the thousands of new laborers flooding into the Portland area to work in the Kaiser shipyards. Many of these new workers were Black. Shoddy housing went up and the new town of Vanport appeared on a flood plane of the Columbia River between Portland and Vancouver, Washington.

On the morning of Memorial Day
May 30th, 1948, with waters rising,
the Housing Authority of Portland
issued the following statement:
"Remember: dikes are safe at present.
You will be warned if necessary. You
will have time to leave. Don't get
excited."

That afternoon, at exactly 4:17 PM
the railroad berm broke and the
Columbia went tearing through Vanport,
lifting badly built dwellings up in the
air on a rush of current, uprooting trees,
swirling cars through the streets,
drowning the innocent, destroying lives.

The rescue response was swift. Many rushed to high ground, some formed human chains, boats were dispatched to collect survivors. Many people were away from home for the holiday. The official death toll ~ a ~ round ten people ~ was staggeringly low. Whispers of much higher number counts abounded.

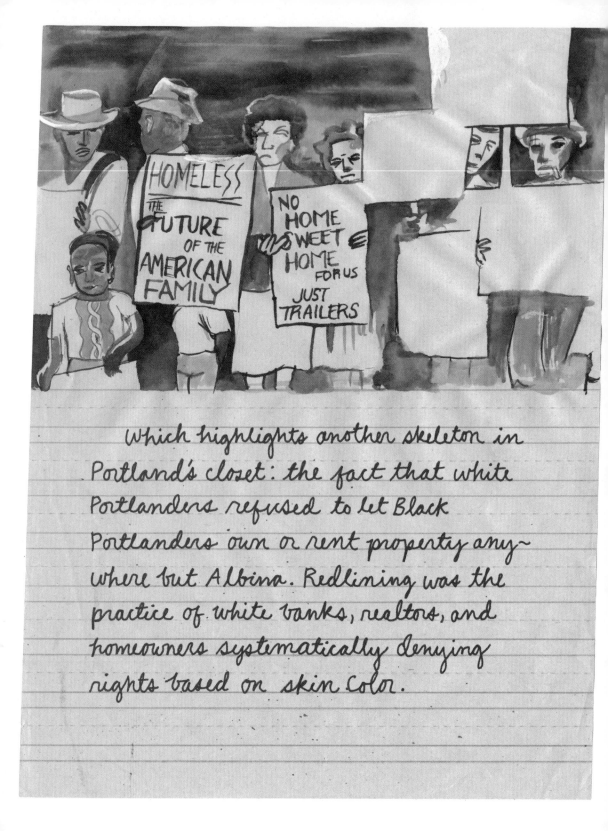

Which highlights another skeleton in Portland's closet: the fact that white Portlanders refused to let Black Portlanders own or rent property any~ where but Albina. Redlining was the practice of white banks, realtors, and homeowners systematically denying rights based on skin color.

Many Portlanders welcomed Vanport refugees into their homes (though I am sure many did not). For the rest, temp~ orary trailers were set up. But thousands were left essentially homeless. Many of the Black Vanport residents relocated to the Albina neighborhood.

Despite efforts toward its demise, Albina managed to remain a thriving community for decades. The question remains whether the community can weather this most recent wave of settler colonialism. My family arrived there in 1978. My parents had driven west until the money ran out in Portland. We had a home because we were white. The home was haunted, chaotic, unsafe. But it was home.

A few years ago Alder called to tell me there was a New Year's Eve party happening at the old house and wouldn't it be weird to go? I had been crying all day for reasons I'd rather not go into, and it did sound weird so I went. And it was weird. I felt the ghosts talking to me. Who are all these fashionable people danc~ing in the living room? It's too loud, they said. I walked away but they kept talking.

On the night of March 12, 1981, several blocks away from our house, officers Craig Ward and Jim Galloway dumped a pile of dead possums on the doorstep of the Burger Barn, a popular Black-owned restaurant on what was then Union Avenue.

Witnesses reported several officers total involved in the "possum incident". The Black community in Albina took to the streets against the harassment. Ward and Galloway were fired. Police officers assembled and marched in counter-protest. Ward and Galloway were rehired to their posts.

Down the street from our house, near the Lloyd Center Mall on April 21st, 1985, Lloyd D. "Tony" Stevenson, a security guard, karate expert, marine, and father of five, was strangled to death by officer Gary L. Barbour. The death was a result of Barbour's use of the carotid artery hold, or "choke" hold.

To add insult to injury, two Portland police officers released T-shirts on the morning of Stevenson's funeral that read, "Don't choke 'em... smoke 'em." The officers who made the shirts were fired, but later reinstated. The Stevenson murder would presage other more recent and wider publicized police murders.

Tony Stevenson was trying to subdue a shoplifting suspect when he got into an altercation with a witness. Officer Barbour, arriving on the scene, incorrectly identified Stevenson as the perpetrator. Barbour was white, Stevenson was Black.

The Albina community erupted in anger. Crowds of protestors marched and amassed outside the home of Portland police chief Charles Moose, near Irving Park. Police fought the community back with bean bag bullets and mace.

The murder of Kendra James by the Portland police in 2003 hit me hard. She was my age, we grew up in the same neighborhood. White privilege and racism varied our life paths exponentially.

Kendra was shot and killed by officer Scott McCollister during a traffic stop on North Skidmore. She was 27 years old and is survived by two children.

The response from the Albina
community was swift and fierce. We
took to the streets. We marched for
justice, not peace. The community was
in pain.

It is impossible to quantify the damage these events cause, the echoing ripples. I'm choosing to repeat these events here to add to the din of voices refusing to let them be forgotten.

James "jim jim" Chasse was beaten to death by cops in 2006, 3 years after Kendra was Killed. He was schizophrenic and homeless when he tried to run from the cops who Killed him. Many years earlier Jim Jim was immortalized in a Portland punk single, "Alien Boy" by the Wipers. Chasse went to M.L.C., like me.

Three years later, Chris Humphreys, one of the officers responsible for the death of James Chasse, emptied a round of bean~ bag bullets into the body of a twelve-year~old Black girl. When he was put on leave, police offi~ cers marched en masse wearing "I am Chris Humphreys" T-shirts.

In 2010, police captain Mark Kruger was suspended without pay after having erected a plaque to five nazi-era German soldiers on a tree at Rocky Butte. Old friends came forward to admit they had been nazis with Kruger. Youtube videos emerged of Kruger sporting nazi garb.

Kruger served on duty through the Kendra James and James Chasse murders and the bean bag incident. He is known to loathe radical leftists and protesters. He was promoted to captain of the Portland drug and vice division. In 2014, Kruger was reimbursed by the city for money lost during his suspension, and his discipline record erased.

In January 2018, the Bundys walked free after a federal judge dismissed the Malheur County stand-off case. There were no penalties for their armed occupation. And remember the Hammonds~ the arsonists all this fuss was over in the first place? This July they rode home from prison in style~ on a private jet owned by a friend of Mike Pence~ after receiving a pardon from President Trump.

In 2008, a nazi flag attached to a four-foot balloon greeted morning commuters crossing the Fremont Bridge in Portland, Oregon.

Oregon did not begin well, nor does this story end well. White supremacy is written into Oregon's foundations, with no sign of crumbling. Fortunately, there has always been and will always be resistance.

CHAPTER 4

Victims
of
Groupthink

River Phoenix lay dying out in front of the Viper Room in the early hours of October 31st, 1993. Halloween 2020 marked the 27th anniversary of his death.

River's sister Rain flung herself onto her brother's body in an effort to control the convulsions. Joaquin was at a near-by pay phone, begging the operator for an ambulance, pleading with them to hurry. "Please come, he's dying, please." This is how many of us were introduced to Joaquin: his terrified voice on the nightly news.

The first time I can re-member seeing Joaquin Phoenix was in Gus Van Sant's "To Die For", inspired by the true story of Pamela Smart. This is one of Gus's only films where a creepy, older character is portrayed as an actual predator. And I guess she just hap-pened to be a woman.

In 2005, Joaquin was nom~
inated for an Oscar for his role in
the Johnny Cash biopic, "Walk the Line".
As Cash, Joaquin was playing someone
who had also witnessed the tragic
death of an older brother.

That night, Johnny Depp was playing a set with his band "P". Onstage were Depp, Flea, Depp's business partner Sal Jenco, Gibby Haynes of the Butthole Surfers, Al Jourgensen of Ministry, and Benmont Tench of Tom Petty and the Heartbreakers.

River and Flea had been close buds
since their days spent jamming together
at Gus's house during the filming of "My
Own Private Idaho." River was also particularly
tight with Chili Pepper guitarist John
Frusciante. Leading up to that night at the
Viper Room the two were said to have been
consuming massive amounts of heroin & cocaine.

That night, "P" was playing a song called "Michael Stipe", reportedly while River Phoenix convulsed outside. The lyrics went, "I finally talked to Michael Stipe/But I didn't get to see his car/Him and River Phoenix/Were leaving on the road tomorrow."

River idolized the Red Hot Chili Peppers. They were nearing their height of fame with the album "Blood Sugar Sex Magik", complete with photographs and art direction by Gus Van Sant.

Another song to name~drop River
is the Red Hot Chili Peppers' "Give it Away":
"There's a River, born to be a giver
Keep you warm, won't let you shiver
His heart is never gonna wither
Come on everybody time to deliver."

The Chili Peppers' song "Under the Bridge", about using heroin in L.A., was released in 1991. The music video was directed by Gus Van Sant and features clips of Portland skyline and bridges.

Bob Forrest of the band Thelonious Monster claims to have encountered River on that fateful night. "Bob, I don't feel so good," said River. "I think I'm OD'ing." Forrest dismissed him. After the event, he, Flea, Johnny Depp, and the rest of the gang left town to avoid any scadalous implications.

The Phoenix family strongly did not want anyone else taking the fall for the drugs River did. At River's memorial service, the Phoenix clan took turns describing him as too good for this world and pondering how he had progressed to a higher state of being.

Actress Martha Plimpton (River's friend and ex) described the scene: "You would have thought he was 90 and died in his sleep. I don't want to be comforted by his death. I think it's right that I'm angry about it, angry at the people who helped him stay sick, and angry at River."

In 1901, the North Pacific Sanitorium began operating out of the old Levi White residence. After an outbreak of smallpox the structure was torn down. In 1914 a new building, the Couch School, was erected on its foundations.

In 1968, an experimental program was implemented at Couch School called the Metropolitan Learning Center, or M.L.C. Students were encouraged to plan and choose their own curricula, and call teachers by their first names. There was lots of mixing across age groups and there were no grades.

By the time I arrived there in the '80s, M.L.C. had become the whole school. I remember the tenet of "question authority" being strongly upheld. Just because an adult says it, does not make it a fact. Extreme ideas and radical ideologies cropped up among the student body. The lack of adult supervision also meant that budding nazis Ken Mieske and Steve Strasser could be overlooked.

M.L.C. saw its share of death. The year before I arrived a student plunged to their death off a cliff at the coast. Ziggy died in the shop, leaving a great hole and a school full of mourners. Abe was found in the river. Will died of a heart three sizes too big. Molly took her own life. So did Kojo, and Minh. Those are people who died.

When the Oregon Episcopal
School disaster occured in 1986, M.L.C.
claimed a few ex~students as survivors.
A rumor went up that they'd survived
because they questioned authority, that
they'd turned back when conditions on
the mountain grew treacherous, despite
the urgings~on of the adult in charge.
The others who did not, died.

It was the eve of Mother's Day, May 12th, 1986, when they set out hours before dawn. 13 hikers heading into one of the greatest outdoor disasters in Oregon history. Ten students, two teachers, and a guide awaited rescue in a snow cave. Only three survived. Some of their party had turned back earlier. A beloved teacher pressed the rest on. It was a rite of passage, he insisted.

I had a chance meeting once with a survivor, one of the boys who turned back early on. I asked him why he turned back. He was an ex-M.L.C. student. So were the rumors true? He answered that yes, Thomas Goman, school chaplain and expedition leader, was acting belligerant and pressuring them to summit the mountain despite the oncoming storm.

But it was this survivor's stomach, and a little teenage fancy, that sealed his fate and brought him down the mountain alive; he got diarrhea. Maybe from fear or maybe altitude sickness, but the thought of being sick in front of his girl-crush sent him packing. He said it flashed in his mind that he didn't give a damn about scaling a mountain if it meant dying before his first blowjob.

Searchers found the cave late in the day, May 14th. Only three people survived, a boy and a girl who were close to the top of the pile of bodies, as well as their guide who had gotten out and found help. Three other bodies were found on the slopes outside the cave, nine dead total. In an official in~quest it was determined that Goman was (posthumously) significantly to blame for the tragedy.

In 6th grade, we went to Outdoor school. We were shipped out to the forest for a week with three other schools: Ockley Green, Hosford, and Whitaker. With M.L.C., these were all "bad" schools. Why had they put us all together; was it some sort of social experiment?

And so it seemed when we arrived. There was a strictness and a harsh vibe we weren't used to. The Whitaker and Ockley Green girls complained of racism from the teen-aged camp counselors. Homesick kids cried themselves to sleep at night.

Us kids knew we'd been had in the name of "science". Most of what we learned out there was fur~ ther proof that grown ups could not be trusted.

Whitaker had a tough row to hoe. They had a reputation as one of the worst schools in the district. In terms of low test scores, behavioral infractions, and excessive absences, Whitaker outdid all the other middle schools in Portland.

In the year 2001, the news broke
that the Whitaker School building had
been found to be emitting dangerously
high levels of radon gas. Coupled with
bad ventilation, this was enough to explain
everything from teacher's absences and
workers comp claims to low test scores and
behavioral issues. The school district
had known of the situation for ten years
without alerting students, teachers, or families.

The students were bussed to other school districts and Whitaker closed its doors for good. Just before the building was razed, Gus Van Sant opted to film his movie "Elephant" there. "There is no pumped-up style, no lingering, no release, no climax. Just implacable, poker-faced, flat, uninfected death." ~ Roger Ebert on "Elephant."

Whitaker's swan song is a school shooting reenactment devoid of empathy or any real feelings of any kind. Roger Ebert called the movie's creation a "brave and radical act." Other reviews called it "pointless at best and irresposible at worst."

Van Sant told Roger Ebert at Cannes Film Festival, "I want the audience to make its own observations and draw its own conclusions. Who knows why those boys acted as they did?" Yeah. Who knows?

Macheesmo Mouse was an unfortu~ nately named "healthy" faux~mexican food chain in the Portland area during the '90s and early aughts. Alder worked there when we were teenagers. They had menu items like "global wrap" and had margaritas on tap.

Tiger Warren was the big cheese of this operation, and pal of Gus Van Sant. Warren can be seen in his cameo in "My Own Private Idaho" where he plays himself. Our Macheesmo Mouse had a few paintings by Van Sant on the walls. They were ethereal cartoony landscapes reminiscent of the visionary sequences in "Drugstore Cowboy" and "Idaho".

In November 1999, the plane Tiger Warren was piloting plunged into the Columbia River Gorge, killing Tiger and his three sons. Tiger had recently testified against his friend Daniel Jenkins. Jenkins asked Tiger for help hiring a hitman to kill Tiger's ex~wife's new husband. Jenkins was con~victed. Eight days later Tiger and his sons were dead.

On a freezing cold night, December 28th, 1978, United Airlines flight 173 crashes down on 157th and East Burnside in a suburban neighborhood, killing ten. My mom is just about to go into labor with me.

RESTRICTED AREA
KEEP OUT
NATIONAL TRANSPORTATION
SAFETY BOARD

All was still well as the airplane approached Portland International Airport around 5:30 PM. Then the landing gear was deployed and two great ker-whams were heard and felt, rocking the aircraft. They circled the airport for an hour trying to determine the problem. Then they abruptly ran out of gas.

"We're going down. We're not going to make the airport." The first officer radioed in a mayday. He would not survive the crash. Captain McBroom brought the failing aircraft down in a dark area he hoped was a park. The plane leveled two houses that were miraculously uninhabited at the time. The question remained: How did this happen?

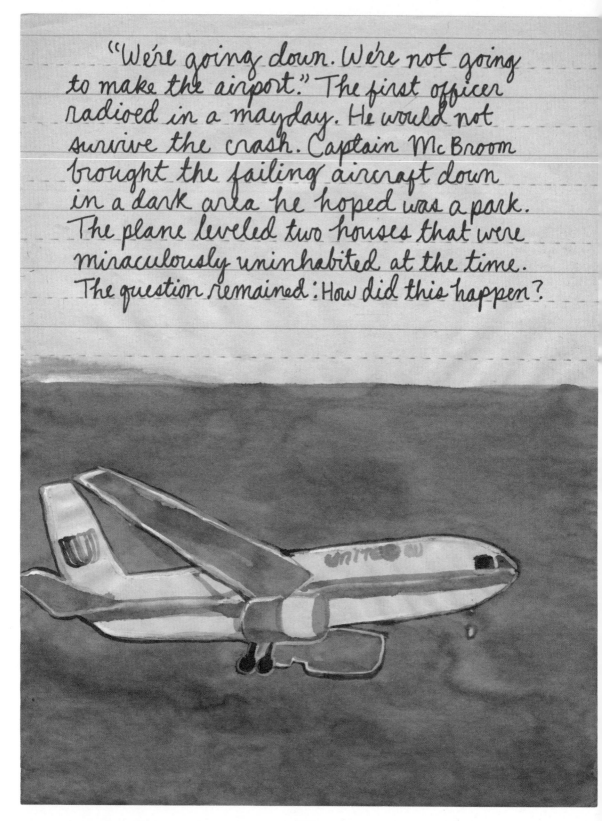

The responsibility was placed
squarely on the shoulders of Captain
McBroom and the old boys' cockpit
culture of top-dog behavior on the
part of the pilots. The event and the
trial that followed helped implement
vast changes in cockpit practices that
are still in place today. Questioning
power is encouraged. The top-down
paradigm is deconstructed. The culture
is changed.

Groupthink is a phenomenon wherein small, cohesive groups of people go bad, often in the name of the good of the small group. Irving Janis analyzes this phenomena in his seminal, "Victims of Groupthink", examining past governmental and military SNAFUs and isolating the groupthink dynamics of different disasters. He then offers solutions to typical groupthink pitfalls.

One way to combat groupthink is to have rotating leadership; small groups are more likely to succumb to groupthink if there is a set authority figure within the group. Another way is to encourage dissent; a group that can speak out in the face of bad leadership is a healthy group. The analytics of how to combat groupthink have been applied to cockpit dynamics at the highest levels, benefiting airline travellers.

In her 2003 landmark exposé, "One Hundred Little Hitlers," Elinor Langer interviews Mr. X about Ken Death's budding racist views. "How can Black people talk about Black Pride and be separatist and that's OK but when white people just want to hang out together they're called racists?" To which Mr. X says he never found a good answer. Major fail, Mr. X.

We fail young people every day. Kids need adults they can trust to explain the hard realities of institutional oppression. That there is no such thing as reverse racism. Or that age difference can result in power imbalance.

If Ken Death hadn't died in prison he would be up for release. I shudder to think of how he might have been received by white nation-alists. His cohort Kyle Brewster has been spotted sleeping on the porch of a local neo-nazi hangout.

Their mentor Tom Metzger still makes appearances at rallies full of alt-right types, mostly young neo-nazis, proud boys, patriot player, etc.

In closing, here are some words from an open letter penned by River Phoenix's mother Heart, published in the L.A. Times: "It is my prayer that River's leaving in this way will focus the attention of the world on how painfully the spirits of his generation are being worn down... if River's passing opens our global heart then I say thanks, dear, beloved son, for yet another gift to all of us."

EPILOGUE

Young Hatemongers

EPILOGUE

Young Hofmannn

When I was researching
the second chapter I made a
chilling discovery while slow-
motion viewing the November
1988 episode of the Geraldo Rivera
show, titled "Young Hatemongers"
on Youtube.

It was the riot episode, the one
where Geraldo has his nose broken
by a flying chair. Onstage were three
white supremacists saying horrible
things. It made for great ratings.
In one of the stills I notice the
back of a man's head and I recog-
nize him. I know that greasy black
hair with the blond roots because
I've been drawing it for the past
few weeks!

It was Ken "Death" Mieske, the ringleader of the racist murder of Mulugeta Seraw. I had spent years trying to find film footage of him, and here he was on "Geraldo"? Ten days after shooting this episode, Ken was committing a murder in Portland. What the hell was he doing in New York City?

There on his left was his girlfriend, Julie Belec. A vehement racist at this time, we see Julie roll her eyes and sneer throughout the episode. We hear her heckle the skinheads onstage for not being radical enough. She seems to be trying to provoke them.

Which gives credence to some people's claims that Julie was more a part of things than she led us to believe. She was in the car. It's not hard to imagine her egging Ken on to attack two men she equated with subhumans. She made herself look pretty awful on "Geraldo."

The episode raised the bar for tasteless television. It also unwittingly became a catalyst for the "coming out" of radical white supremacists who viewed the program as fuel for their racist ideologies.

It may also indicate something even more sinister. The very next night, after watching themselves on TV, four young neo-nazis got drunk and killed Mulugeta Seraw. After being broad~ cast on national TV heckling a skinhead leader for discouraging shows of skinhead violence celebrating the 50th anniversary of Kristallnacht.

Among the guests assembled onstage was Roy Innis, chairman of the Congress of Racial Equality. Here, Geraldo places a paternalistic hand on Innis's shoulder.

On the other side of the
stage sat a sneering John
Metzger, accompanied by two
skinhead goons. He'd brought them
to provide provocation & they delivered.

Rabbi A. Bruce Goldman was seated next to Roy Innis and brought a radical leftist viewpoint to the table.

while Julie sneered
and Ken gave good face.

John Metzger and his goons do all they can to raise the ire of the audience and really piss off their host.

Geraldo would be praised on the internet~to~come for his performance in the riot, where his skills at boxing came in handy.

The riot was arguably started by John Metzger about halfway through the program. Things were not escalating to his liking so out of the flue he began hurling racist slurs. It was not long before Innis lost his cool.

Which led to about a dozen
skinheads hopping up onstage and
beating heads. One brawny skin~
head picks up a chair and chucks it
at Geraldo, breaking his nose.

When things finally calm down, the offending skinheads are shuffled out of the building. Are they being arrested? Nope, the police are just escorting the neo-nazis into a van waiting to take them back to their hotel. "Ladies and gentlemen, New York's finest!" Geraldo quips, obviously annoyed.

Upon slowing down the footage, one can see that something suspicious is afoot. In the moments just before the riot begins you can see Ken slowly rise up in the foreground. He makes hard eye contact with someone offscreen to his left. The skin on the left side of the stage follows Ken's gaze, then snaps back to Ken. It all happens in a matter of seconds.

I watch Ken assume a drill sergeant pose and yell something that makes the other skins go wild. They leap into the pit from all sides of the stage. Ken, in his meaty thickness, hardly wavers, except to flash hand signals to his eager minions. He is a maestro. The riot is his symphony. Then, through the pixelated haze I spot a familiar toupeé.

It's Metzger Senior, right there in the center of the melee. I'd taken him for security — except that it appears Geraldo had none. Tom Metzger, who Morris Dees and the Southern Poverty Law Center took to the mat to prove a connection of any kind between himself and the Killer Mieske — here it was all along.

To his credit, Geraldo wipes the blood out of his ears and eyes and continues taping the episode, broken nose and all. After most of the skinheads have left the building, Ken pesters Geraldo into an interview, while his remaining pals cringe in horror. Ken had a plan. A message to deliver.

What may sound to some like a barely comprehensible anti-fascist tirade is really an encoded message to the other skins. Mieske insists that _his_ people are the minority (meaning punk skins who aren't afraid to use violence). His sentences ramble, but his face shows his terrifying conviction.

Innis ends his piece with eerie irony, calling Ken, Julie, and their friends "good kids". By this time Ken has somehow endeared himself to everyone in the room. Rabbi Goldman ended in this way: "Do you know what a nazi looks like? He looks like your own uncle. He looks like our neighbor mowing the lawn!"

Julie's eyes roll so far back into her head I think they might roll out. In later interviews Julie would point to her upbringing. "There was never any parental direction that this was not a good choice. In my whole growing up, I could not look to my parents for advice on anything. When you are a teenager you really need someone directing your choices. Without that there, I made horrible decisions."

Rabbi Goldman continues: "He could have a shaven head, or he could have long hair. He can wear a three piece suit." Or a gun, with a hat and a badge.

Fin

Bibliography

· Associated Press. Transcript of the four-minute 911 emergency call to the County Fire Department by Joaquin Rafael "Leaf" Phoenix, brother of River Phoenix, after the actor collapsed outside a nightclub, 1993.

· Blalock, Barney. Portland's Lost Waterfront. The History Press, 2012.

· Chandler, J.D. Hidden History of Portland, Oregon. The History Press, 2013.

· Chandler, J.D. Murder & Mayhem in Portland, Oregon. The History Press, 2013.

· Curtis, Walt. Mala Noché. Bridge City Books, 1977, 1997.

· Dietrich, William. Northwest Passage: The Great Columbia River. University of Washington Press, 1995.

· Drury, Clifford M. Marcus and Narcissa Whitman and the Opening of Old Oregon, Volumes 1 & 2. Northwest Interpretive Association, 1986, 1994.

· Ebert, Roger. Elephant-Review. rogerebert.com, Nov. 7, 2003

- Edwards, Gavin. *Last Night at the Viper Room: River Phoenix and the Hollywood He Left Behind*. It Books, 2013.
- Forrest, Bob. *Running With Monsters*. Crown Archetype, 2013.
- Imarisha, Walidah. *Why Aren't There More Black People in Oregon? A public lecture*, 2014~present.
- Intelligence Report. *Lessons and Regrets: Two Decades Later a Woman Remembers Her Life Among Killer Skinheads and Discusses How She Has Changed*. Interview with Julie Belec by Southern Poverty Law Center, March 2, 2010.
- Jaquiss, Nigel. *The Poisoning of Whitaker*. Willamette Week, May 22, 2001.
- Janis, Irving. *Victims of Groupthink*. Houghton Mifflin Company, 1972.
- Langer, Elinor. *One Hundred Little Hitlers: The Death of a Black Man, the Trial of a White Racist, and the Rise of the Neo-Nazi Movent in America*. Metropolitan Books, 2003.

• MacColl, E. Kimbark. The Growth of a city: Power and Politics in Portland, Oregon 1915 to 1950. The Georgian Press, 1979.

• McCarthy, Todd. Elephant ~ Review. Variety Magazine, May 18, 2003.

• Oregon Historical Society. The Oregon History Project. org.

• Parish, James Robert. Gus Van Sant: An Unauthorized Biography. Thunder's Mouth Press, 2001.

• Redden, Jim. The Faces of Death: Street Kid, Actor, Musician, Skinhead ~ Who is the Real Kenneth Murray Mieske? Willamette Week, Dec. 1, 1988.

• Sager, Catherine, Elizabeth, and Matilda. The Whitman Massacre of 1847. Ye Galleon Press, reprinted 1997.

• Stanford, Phil. Portland Confidential: Sex, Crime, and Corruption in the Rose City. PTown Books, 2004.

• Toutonghi, Pauls. Mt. Hood's Deadliest Disaster.

Outside Magazine, Nov. 1, 2018.
• Van Sant, Gus. My Own Private Idaho [screenplay and interview]. Faber and Faber, 1993.
• Willamette Week. Ken "Death" Mieske Dies. July 17, 2011.
• Whipple, Julie. Crash Course: Accidents Don't just happen. Yamhill Canyon Press, 2018.

Videos and Movies

• Arresting Power: Resisting Police Violence in Portland, Oregon, 2014.
• Drugstore Cowboy, Gus Van Sant. 1989
• The Final 24 ~ River Phoenix. 2015. youtube.com
• Good Skinheads, Bad Skinheads, and the Lone Neo~Nazi [the Oprah skinhead episode as seen on youtube.com]. 1988
• Hate on Trial With Bill Moyers. 1992.
• Local Color: Oregon's Forgotten History. PBS, 1999.
• Mala Noche, Gus Vant Sant. 1986

- My Own Private Idaho, Gus Van Sant. 1991.
- No Skin off My Ass, Bruce LaBruce. 1991
- Portland Civil Rights: Lift Ev'ry Voice. 2015
- Streetwise, Martin Bell. 1984.
- To Die For, Gus Van Sant. 1995.
- Why Aren't There More Black People in Oregon? A Hidden History. by Walidah Imarisha. 2014. youtube.com.
- Elephant, Gus Van Sant. 2003.
- Young Hatemongers: Episode of the Geraldo Rivera Show, 1988. youtube.com.

Thanks to Dr. Darell Millner, professor emeritus at Portland State University, without whose invaluable scholarship parts of this book wouldn't exist.
Thanks to all the people at Fantagraphics who helped make this book what it is.

Special thanks to: Stephen R. Bissette, Cathy Camper, Neelybat Chestnut, Robert Clough, Brandon Elston, Austin English, Tim Goodyear, Bill Kartalopoulos, Robert Kirby, Annie Koyama, Jason T. Miles, Donna Murphy, Gardner Murphy, Joe Murphy, Amy Ongiri, John Porcellino, Eric Reynolds, Whit Taylor-Becker, and Alexis Wolf for providing such excellent and helpful feedback, moral support, editorial skills, legal advice, financial support, incisive reviews, distribution help, and for being such a stellar array of voices I respect, throughout this project, thank you.